GOD's *little* INSTRUCTION BOOK

for Grandparents

HONOR
B O O K S

GIFT BOOKS
from Hallmark

BOK4107

REFERENCES

Unless otherwise indicated, all Scripture quotations are taken from the *Holy Bible, New International Version®*. NIV®. Copyright © 1973, 1978, 1984 by International Bible Society. Used by permission of Zondervan Publishing House. All rights reserved.

Scripture quotations marked KJV are taken from the *King James Version* of the Bible.

Scripture quotations marked RSV are from the *Revised Standard Version* of the Bible Copyright © 1946, 1952, and 1971 by the Division of Christian Education of the Churches of Christ in the United States of America. Used by permission. All rights reserved.

Scripture quotations marked NASB are taken from the *New American Standard Bible*. Copyright © The Lockman Foundation 1960, 1962, 1963, 1968, 1971, 1972, 1973, 1975, 1977, 1995. Used by permission.

Scripture quotations marked NKJV are taken from *The New King James Version*. Copyright © 1979, 1980, 1982, Thomas Nelson, Inc.

Scripture quotations marked AMP are taken from *The Amplified Bible. Old Testament* copyright © 1965, 1987 by Zondervan Corporation, Grand Rapids, Michigan. *New Testament* copyright © 1958, 1987 by The Lockman Foundation, La Habra, California. Used by permission.

Scripture quotations marked TLB are taken from *The Living Bible*. Copyright © 1971. Used by permission of Tyndale House Publishers, Inc., Wheaton, Illinois 60189. All rights reserved.

INTRODUCTION

Being a grandparent is one of life's greatest joys. It combines the intensity of unconditional love with the comfort of deferred responsibility. Someone else is in the driver's seat this time, but you have been invited to come along for the ride. What a deal!

At Honor Books, we recognize the unique possibilities and pleasures of the grandparenting experience. Therefore, we have created this little book, *God's Little Instruction Book for Grandparents*, to capture the hopes, joys, and inspiration inherent in this wonderful stage of life.

If you are already a grandparent, you will relate immediately to the simple truths and humorous asides. If you are not yet a grandparent, you will have an opportunity to take a peek at what lies ahead for you.

So sit back and enjoy!

Grandchildren are God's compensation for growing old.

The LORD will guide you always;
he will satisfy your needs.

—Isaiah 58:11

No one is quicker on the draw than a grandparent pulling pictures from a wallet.

Show me your face . . . your face is lovely.
—Song of Songs 2:14

A grandparent is a living history lesson.

I will instruct you and teach you in the way you should go.

Psalm 32:8

What is a grandmother?

Someone who puts a sweater
on you when *she* is cold,
feeds you when *she* is hungry,
and puts you to bed when *she* is tired.

"It is more blessed to give than to receive."
—Acts 20:35

Certain personality traits are thought to skip a generation.

Maybe that's why grandchildren and grandparents get along so well.

You have given me the heritage of those who fear your name.

—Psalm 61:5

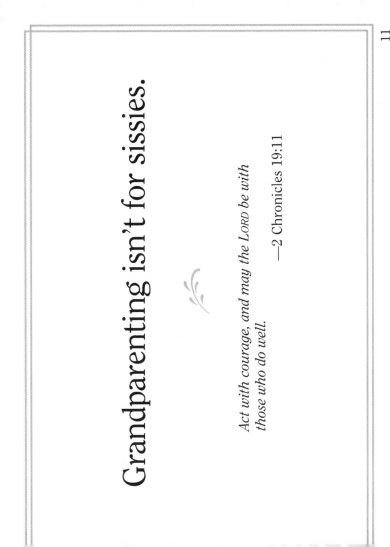

Grandparenting isn't for sissies.

Act with courage, and may the LORD be with those who do well.

—2 Chronicles 19:11

Grandparents should remember:

Unless you're made of cheese,
age doesn't matter.

Children's children are a crown to the aged.

—Proverbs 17:6

Worry is like a rocking chair—it gives you something to do but gets you nowhere.

"Who of you by worrying can add a single hour to his life?"

—Matthew 6:27

If you can't recall
a grandchild's name,
"Dear" or "Sweetie"
will do just fine.

Do everything in love.

—1 Corinthians 16:14

A grandparent is a baby-sitter who watches the kids, not the television.

The LORD watches over all who love him.
—Psalm 145:20

What can even a small child
manipulate easily?
Answer: a grandparent!

*"You have hidden these things from the wise and
learned, and revealed them to little children."*

—Matthew 11:25

Grandparents are folks
who come to your house,
spoil your children,
then go home.

He blesses the home of the righteous.
—Proverbs 3:33

A grandparent remembers
hundreds of "true" stories—
whether they happened or not.

I will remember the deeds of the LORD; yes,
I will remember your miracles of long ago.

—Psalm 77:11

Grandchildren and grandparents get along so well because they often have a common simplicity.

A cord of three strands is not quickly broken.
—Ecclesiastes 4:12

If the old will speak with love,
the young will listen.

A man finds joy in giving an apt reply—
and how good is a timely word!

—Proverbs 15:23

Don't just give your grandchildren good advice; give them good memories.

The memory of the righteous will be a blessing.
—Proverbs 10:7

Toys and teddy bears have no business being in a closet when there are grandkids in the house.

I have seen a grievous evil under the sun: wealth hoarded to the harm of its owner.

—Ecclesiastes 5:13

You may have more grandchildren than you can name but never more than you can love!

"A new command I give you: Love one another. As I have loved you, so you must love one another."

—John 13:34

The quickest way to get
a grandchild's attention is to
sit down and look comfortable.

*Accept one another, then, just as Christ accepted
you, in order to bring praise to God.*

—Romans 15:7

Loving a grandchild is circular:
The more love you give,
the more you get—and the
more you want to give again.

Keep yourselves in God's love as you wait for
the mercy of our Lord Jesus Christ to bring
you to eternal life.

—Jude 1:21

Grandchildren need love—
especially when they
don't deserve it.

Above all these put on love, which binds
everything together in perfect harmony.

—Colossians 3:14 RSV

A hug is a great present,
and it's always returnable.

*May the Lord make your love increase and
overflow for each other.*   —1 Thessalonians 3:12

A grandparent is a builder of dreams, a sculptor of souls.

We speak of God's secret wisdom, a wisdom that has been hidden and that God destined for our glory before time began.

—1 Corinthians 2:7

To a child nurtured by loving grandparents, Heaven doesn't seem like such a faraway place.

Our citizenship is in heaven. And we eagerly await a Savior from there.

—Philippians 3:20

A grandparent is a sustaining influence in a child's life and a forever love in a child's heart.

Encourage one another daily, as long as it is called Today.

—Hebrews 3:13

Grandma and Grandpa's house:

Where the great are small,
and the small are great.

*"Whoever wishes to become great among you
shall be your servant."*

—Matthew 20:26 NASB

Wrinkles appear where
smiles have been.

A glad heart makes a cheerful countenance.
—Proverbs 15:13 AMP

Grandparents always know
just what to say—even
when it's nothing at all.

*Little children, let us not love in word or speech
but in deed and in truth.*

—1 John 3:18 RSV

The grandchild's creed:
To God, country, and Grandma be true!

A wife of noble character who can find?
Her children arise and call her blessed;
her husband also, and he praises her.

—Proverbs 31:10,28

A grandparent's love comes
straight from the heart.

Above all, love each other deeply, because love
covers over a multitude of sins.

—1 Peter 4:8

The riches stored in a grandparent's heart can never be stolen.

"Store up for yourselves treasures in heaven, where moth and rust do not destroy, and where thieves do not break in and steal. For where your treasure is, there your heart will be also."

—Matthew 6:20-21

A grandparent's eyes see
miracles where others see messes.

Open my eyes to see wonderful things.
—Psalm 119:18 TLB

Keep pouring out kindness and love—
God won't let them run dry.

The righteous giveth and spareth not.
—Proverbs 21:26 KJV

A good example is the best sermon.

He who walks with the wise grows wise.
—Proverbs 13:20

Be young at heart—
even if you're old everywhere else!

A happy heart is good medicine and a cheerful
mind works healing.

—Proverbs 17:22 AMP

Because they were loved by them right from the start, kids love grandparents with all their hearts.

Children are a gift from God; they are his reward.

—Psalm 127:3 TLB

Splashes of a child's laughter,
jokes told all in fun, delicious food
(sometimes too much) shared by everyone.
Words of truth and goodness, warm hugs and
kisses, too—these are grandparents' keepsakes
to cherish their whole lives through.

*All thy children shall be taught of the LORD; and
great shall be the peace of thy children.*

—Isaiah 54:13 KJV

A grandparent is silver hair,
tin ears, a lead bottom,
and a heart of gold.

Gray hair is a crown of splendor; it is attained
by a righteous life.

—Proverbs 16:31

A Poem for Grandma

For the twinkle in Grandma's eyes,
For her tender lullabies,
For all the fun she has in store,
I'll love her always, plus one day more.

*She opens her mouth in skillful and godly
Wisdom, and on her tongue is the law of kindness.*

—Proverbs 31:26 AMP

A Poem for Grandpa

He can pull a nickel from his ear
And tickles me when I get near.
Then he sets me on his knee—
I love my Grandpa, and he loves me!

*Do not withhold good from those who deserve it,
when it is in your power to act.*

—Proverbs 3:27

It's not how old you are;
it's how you are old.

A righteous man who walks in his integrity—
How blessed are his sons after him.

—Proverbs 20:7 NASB

A grandparent's good humor
lightens a grandchild's burdens.

The light in the eyes [of him whose heart is
joyful] rejoices the hearts of others.
—Proverbs 15:30 AMP

A Grandparent's Axiom

Do a good deed.
Sow a good seed.

Whatever is true, whatever is noble, whatever is right, whatever is pure, whatever is lovely, whatever is admirable—if anything is excellent or praiseworthy—think about such things.

—Philippians 4:8

It's memories,
not money,
that make you rich!

"Be on your guard against all kinds of greed; a man's life does not consist in the abundance of his possessions."

—Luke 12:15

If you find your knees knocking, try kneeling on them.

Do not be anxious about anything, but in everything, by prayer and petition, with thanksgiving, present your requests to God. And the peace of God, which transcends all understanding, will guard your hearts and your minds in Christ Jesus.

—Philippians 4:6-7

What's ahead is even better than what's behind.

We are looking forward to a new heaven and a new earth, the home of righteousness.

—2 Peter 3:13

Godly grandparents make life grand.

Your love has given me great joy.

—Philemon 1:7

The heart that loves
is always young.

Many waters cannot quench love, neither can floods drown it.

—Song of Solomon 8:7 RSV

The most important thing
a grandpa can do for his
children and grandchildren
is to love their grandma.

So ought men to love their wives as their own
bodies. He that loveth his wife loveth himself.

—Ephesians 5:28 KJV

Don't believe the experts—
grandpas CAN be domesticated.

With God nothing shall be impossible.
—Luke 1:37 KJV

An ounce of leading by example
is worth a pound of pressure.

*"I have set you an example that you should do
as I have done for you."*

—John 13:15

Put God first,
and your marriage will last.

Let each one of you in particular so love his own wife as himself, and let the wife see that she respects her husband.

—Ephesians 5:33 NKJV

Being a grandparent
can feel like a marathon—
you need perseverance and
good, comfortable shoes.

*Let us run with perseverance the race marked
out for us.*

—Hebrews 12:1

Having grandchildren doubles
joy and divides grief in half.

*If two lie down together, then they have warmth;
but how can one be warm alone?*

—Ecclesiastes 4:11 AMP

Marriage has its low notes
and high notes but, all in all,
it's one sweet song,
especially in the golden years.

I will betroth you to me forever; I will betroth
you in righteousness and justice, in love
and compassion.

—Hosea 2:19

The invariable mark
of wisdom is to see and hear
the miraculous in the common.

Let the wise listen.

—Proverbs 1:5

Work as if you were to live
a hundred years; pray as if
you were to die tomorrow.

Cast your cares on the LORD and he will sustain
you; he will never let the righteous fall.

—Psalm 55:22

As the purse is emptied,
the heart is filled.

God loves a cheerful giver.

—2 Corinthians 9:7

Even mediocre grandparents
are always at their best.

*Those who have served well gain an
excellent standing.*

—1 Timothy 3:13

Love is the world's
most beautiful verb.

*He will quiet you with his love, he will rejoice
over you with singing.*

—Zephaniah 3:17

One advantage of a bad memory is that you can, for the first time, repeatedly enjoy the same joke.

Be patient with each other, making allowance for each other's faults because of your love.

—Ephesians 4:2 TLB

A couple can accomplish much if they don't care who gets the credit.

Do nothing from selfishness or empty conceit, but with humility of mind let each of you regard one another as more important than himself.
—Philippians 2:3 NASB

You make a living by what you get;
you make a life by what you give.

*"Give, and it will be given to you. A good
measure, pressed down, shaken together and
running over, will be poured into your lap.
For with the measure you use, it will be
measured to you."*

—Luke 6:38

Marriage is a union
that should never go on strike.

*May your fountain be blessed, and may you
rejoice in the wife of your youth. . . . may you
ever be captivated by her love.*

—Proverbs 5:18-19

You're never too old to dream.

Though a righteous man falls seven times,
he rises again.

—Proverbs 24:16

Grandma-hood:

when you start turning off the
lights for economical reasons
rather than romantic ones.

Be joyful always.

—1 Thessalonians 5:16

Money can't buy health, happiness,
or what it bought last year.

Wealth is worthless in the day of wrath,
but righteousness delivers from death.

Proverbs 11:4

Train up children in the way
they should go, and walk
there yourself once in a while.

Do not exasperate your children; instead,
bring them up in the training and instruction
of the Lord.

—Ephesians 6:4

Don't put your grandchildren
down—unless it's on
your prayer list.

Honor one another above yourselves.

—Romans 12:10

The world's best face-lift
is a smile.

Rejoice with them that do rejoice.
—Romans 12:15 KJV

To teach is to learn again.

Let the wise listen and add to their learning.

—Proverbs 1:5

Lots of play keeps
your heart young.

"I have come that they may have life, and have it to the full."

—John 10:10

To be a grandparent,
you have to be off your rocker—
and on the move.

*Let us not become weary in doing good, for at
the proper time we will reap a harvest if we do
not give up.*

—Galatians 6:9

Grandma's kisses always leave something
to be desired—
namely, more kisses!

Greet one another with a kiss of love.

—1 Peter 5:14

Wise people speak when
they have something to say;
foolish people speak when
they have to say something.

*Don't talk so much. You keep putting your foot
in your mouth. Be sensible and turn off the flow!*

—Proverbs 10:19 TLB

Too many of Grandma's square meals make for a round Grandpa!

"Therefore I tell you, do not worry about your life, what you will eat. . . . Life is more than food."

—Luke 12:22-23

A helpful reminder for grandparents—
never change a grandbaby's
diapers in midstream.

*"The more lowly your service to others,
the greater you are. To be the greatest,
be a servant."*

Matthew 23:11 TLB

The wise man ages with Grace—or whatever his wife's name is.

Let patience have her perfect work, that ye may be perfect and entire, wanting nothing.

—James 1:4 KJV

Today is the youngest you will be for the rest of your life.

Make the most of every opportunity you have for doing good.

—Ephesians 5:16 TLB

You know you're a grandma when your idea of sexy lingerie is tube socks and a flannel nightie with only eight buttons.

She has no fear of winter for her household, for she has made warm clothes for all of them.

—Proverbs 31:21 TLB

Grandparenting is an heir-raising experience.

Children are an heritage of the LORD.
—Psalm 127:3 KJV

The best time in a grandparent's life is that 12-year span between 55 and 60!

There is a right time for everything.
Ecclesiastes 3:1 TLB

The mind is like
a parachute; it functions
only when you open it.

If any of you lacks wisdom, he should ask God,
who gives generously to all without finding fault,
and it will be given to him.

—James 1:5 KJV

Grandchildren are like
wet cement—whatever falls
on them makes an impression.

*Be very careful, then, how you live—not
as unwise but as wise, making the most
of every opportunity.*

—Ephesians 5:15-16

What every child knows:
If you want something expensive,
ask your grandparents.

*Hope deferred makes the heart sick but a
longing fulfilled is a tree of life.*

—Proverbs 13:12

The two places a child
is always welcome:
church and grandma's house.

*Share with God's people who are in need.
Practice hospitality.*

—Romans 12:13

Grandchildren spell love
T-I-M-E.

Teach us to number our days aright,
that we may gain a heart of wisdom.

—Psalm 90:12

You can't do anything about your ancestors, but you can greatly influence your descendants.

He decreed statutes . . . which he commanded our forefathers to teach their children, so the next generation would know them.

—Psalm 78:5-6

The best way to teach your grandchildren character is to have lots of it around the house.

As for me and my household, we will serve the LORD.

—Joshua 24:15

Grandchildren give us the opportunity to be the grandparents we wished we had when we were young.

Do not conform any longer to the pattern of this world, but be transformed by the renewing of your mind.

—Romans 12:2

Do the things you can, and let
God handle the things you can't.

*"Come to me, all you who are weary and
burdened, and I will give you rest."*

—Matthew 11:28

A grandpa is a man who carries pictures in his wallet, where money used to be.

A good name is to be chosen rather than great riches, Loving favor rather than silver and gold.
—Proverbs 22:1 NKJV

Love means never having to ask,
"Are you going to finish your dessert?"

*Command them to do good, to be rich in good
deeds, and to be generous and willing to share.*

—1 Timothy 6:18

Don't diet together.
Two people should never
be that cranky simultaneously.

*"Blessed are those who hunger and thirst for
righteousness, for they will be filled."*
—Matthew 5:6

"Ten years ago, I had five theories
about being a grandfather.
Now I have five grandchildren
and no theories!"

Do not be wise in your own eyes.

—Proverbs 3:7

Sometimes the best
conversation you can have
with your grandchild
requires no words.

He who holds his tongue is wise. —Proverbs 10:19

Relationships don't
keep well in cold silence
or heated arguments.

*In your anger do not sin: Do not let the sun go
down while you are still angry.*

—Ephesians 4:26

Today it costs more
to entertain a grandchild
than it did to educate his parents.

He who pursues righteousness and love finds life,
prosperity and honor.

—Proverbs 21:21

A dad is a guy who gives his daughter away to a man who isn't good enough so they can give him grandchildren who are better than anybody's.

There is surely a future hope for you, and your hope will not be cut off.

—Proverbs 23:18

The strongest and sweetest songs
are yet to be sung.

*He put a new song in my mouth, a hymn of
praise to our God.*

—Psalm 40:3

Hearts become wings
when they are opened by love.

Be imitators of God, as beloved children; and
walk in love, just as Christ also loved you, and
gave Himself up for us.

—Ephesians 5:1-2 NASB

Knowledge is a treasure meant to be shared.

Gold there is, and rubies in abundance, but lips that speak knowledge are a rare jewel.

—Proverbs 20:15

It's best to face life as
a team, even if your team
is losing for the moment.

Two can accomplish more than twice as much
as one, for the results can be much better.

—Ecclesiastes 4:9 TLB

Real love means letting
your grandchild
choose the pizza toppings.

*Better a meal of vegetables where there is love
than a fattened calf with hatred.*

—Proverbs 15:17

Grade school teaches
children the facts;
Grandpa teaches them the truth.

I have chosen the way of truth; I have set my heart on your laws.

—Psalm 119:30

If the theory of evolution is valid, why do grandmas have only two hands?

Whatever your hand finds to do, do it with all your might.

—Ecclesiastes 9:10

Grandchildren are
a great help in your old age—
they help you get there faster!

I urge you to live a life worthy of the calling you have received.

—Ephesians 4:1

Grandpa has his will,
but Grandma has her way.

*How delightful is your love, my sister, my bride!
How much more pleasing is your love than
wine, and the fragrance of your perfume than
any spice!*

—Song of Songs 4:10

If you tell the truth,
you don't have to
remember so much.

Truthful lips endure forever.

—Proverbs 12:19

Make sure everything in your house is either useful, beautiful, or delicious.

You will be happy and it will be well with you.
Your wife shall be like a fruitful vine, Within
your house, Your children like olive plants
Around your table.

—Psalm 128:2-3 NASB

A grandparent grows in
stature every time he or she
kneels to help a child.

*"Blessed are the merciful, for they will be
shown mercy."*

—Matthew 5:7

A grandparent can add a great deal to a child's life by providing a gentle hug, an approving smile, or a simple compliment.

As we have opportunity, let us do good to all people, especially to those who belong to the family of believers.

—Galatians 6:10

Children rarely respond to long speeches.
A stern glance or brief comment is often
much more effective,
especially from a grandparent.

*The commandment is a lamp; and the law is
light; and reproofs of instruction are the way
of life.*

—Proverbs 6:23 KJV

Tender moments and lasting memories are most often the result of sharing simple things.

I have learned, in whatsoever state I am, therewith to be content.

—Philippians 4:11 KJV

You know you're a grandparent when your idea of great fun is a school play, a good camera, and plenty of film.

Never be lacking in zeal, but keep your spiritual fervor, serving the Lord.

—Romans 12:11

If you want to spend more time with your grandchild, find a hobby to share.

Whatever you do, work at it with all your heart, as working for the Lord, not for men.
—Colossians 3:23

All children know that a grandparent is someone who greets you with a smile even when everyone else is frowning.

He who covers over an offense promotes love, but whoever repeats the matter separates close friends.

—Proverbs 17:9

It's important to treat your grandchildren
as individuals
with distinctly different personalities,
talents, and abilities.

*Now the body is not made up of one part but of
many. . . . God has arranged the parts in the
body, every one of them, just as he wanted
them to be.*

—1 Corinthians 12:14,18

Grandparents are people
who can afford to make
jokes at their own expense.

*He will yet fill your mouth with laughter and
your lips with shouts of joy.*

—Job 8:21

There are many ways to measure success. For a grandparent it comes down to how your grandchildren describe you to their friends.

As water reflects a face, so a man's heart reflects the man.

—Proverbs 27:19

One of the most important
parts of a grandparent's job
is to nurture self-esteem.

*"Are not five sparrows sold for two pennies?
Yet not one of them is forgotten by God.
Indeed, the very hairs of your head are all
numbered. Don't be afraid; you are worth
more than many sparrows."*

—Luke 12:6-7

Stay alert!
Even infants have been known
to outsmart their grandparents.

The LORD protects the simplehearted.

—Psalm 116:6

Every good grandparent
knows that too much love
has never spoiled a child.

We loved you dearly—so dearly that we gave
you not only God's message, but our own
lives too.

—1 Thessalonians 2:8 TLB

Every good grandparent knows
that giving children everything
they want is a good way
to make them miserable.

*The rod and reproof give wisdom: but a child left
to himself bringeth . . . shame.*

—Proverbs 29:15 KJV

When you feel like you just have to say something—that's the most important time to hold your tongue.

Everyone should be quick to listen, slow to speak and slow to become angry.

—James 1:19

Becoming a grandparent is much easier than *being* a grandparent.

Listen to advice and accept instruction, and in the end you will be wise.

—Proverbs 19:20

The best grandparents are those who have not lost their sense of childlike wonder.

"I tell you the truth, anyone who will not receive the kingdom of God like a little child will never enter it."

—Mark 10:15

Our grandchildren give us a second chance to do the things we wish we had done with our own children.

We know that all things work together for good to them that love God, to them who are the called according to his purpose.

—Romans 8:28 KJV

Grandchildren need
your time—especially when
they don't deserve it!

*Above all, love each other deeply, because love
covers over a multitude of sins.*

—1 Peter 4:8

Measure wealth not by the things you have, but by the things you have for which you would not take money.

"What good will it be for a man if he gains the whole world, yet forfeits his soul?"

—Matthew 16:26

Play with your grandchildren.
They'll teach you how to
be young again.

May the LORD bless you from Zion all the days
of your life; may you see the prosperity of
Jerusalem, and may you live to see your
children's children.

—Psalm 128:5-6

There are two priceless gifts
we can give our grandchildren:
the first is roots;
the other is wings.

If the root is holy, so are the branches.
—Romans 11:16

It takes a long time to become young.

Those who hope in the LORD will renew their strength. They will soar on wings like eagles; they will run and not grow weary, they will walk and not be faint.

—Isaiah 40:31

The pleasure of any activity is doubled when shared with a grandchild.

My people will receive a double portion, and instead of disgrace they will rejoice in their inheritance; and so they will inherit a double portion in their land, and everlasting joy will be theirs.

—Isaiah 61:7

A grandchild's feet may leave your home—but never your heart!

How can we thank God enough for you in return for all the joy we have in the presence of our God because of you? Night and day we pray most earnestly that we may see you again.

—1 Thessalonians 3:9-10

Life is more about moments
than about milestones.

Make the most of every opportunity.
—Colossians 4:5

There's more to being a grandparent than merely having grandchildren.

Be kind to one another, tenderhearted, forgiving one another, as God in Christ forgave you.

—Ephesians 4:32 RSV

A happy childhood is one of
the best gifts grandparents
can give their grandchildren.

May the righteous be glad and rejoice before
God; may they be happy and joyful.
—Psalm 68:3

It's okay for grandparents
to joke around; after all,
every family tree needs a little sap.

Do not be overrighteous, neither be overwise—
why destroy yourself?

—Ecclesiastes 7:16

A grandchild is fed with cookies, milk, and praise.

Pleasant words are as a honeycomb, sweet to the soul, and health to the bones.

—Proverbs 16:24 KJV

A Godly grandparent understands what a child does not say.

He took the children in his arms, put his hands on them and blessed them.

—Mark 10:16

Grandchildren are likely to live up to what you believe of them.

Be their ideal; let them follow the way you teach and live; be a pattern for them in your love, your faith, and your clean thoughts.

—1 Timothy 4:12 TLB

Grandparenting is a partnership with God.

Children are a gift from God;
they are his reward.

—Psalm 127:3 TLB

Rules for Grandparents:

Never correct or criticize
your grandchildren's parents
in front of them.

Do not speak evil of one another, brethren.
—James 4:11 NKJV

Rules for Grandparents:
Always keep your promises!

Like clouds and wind without rain is a man who boasts of gifts he does not give.

—Proverbs 25:14

Rules for Grandparents:

Never interfere when it comes to discipline.

CHILDREN, obey your parents in the Lord: for this is right.

—Ephesians 6:1 KJV

Rules for Grandparents:
Always be honest.

*A good man is known by his truthfulness;
a false man by deceit and lies.*

—Proverbs 12:17 TLB

Rules for Grandparents:

Never make a promise before you check with your grandchild's parents.

Now it is required that those who have been given a trust must prove faithful.

—1 Corinthians 4:2

Rules for Grandparents:

Always let your grandchildren know you love them just the way they are.

Accept one another, then, just as Christ accepted you, in order to bring praise to God.

—Romans 15:7

Rules for Grandparents:

Never encourage your grandchildren to disregard their parent's rules.

A fool spurns his father's discipline, but whoever heeds correction shows prudence.

—Proverbs 15:5

Rules for Grandparents:

Always take time to listen to and encourage your grandchildren.

Encourage one another and build each other up, just as in fact you are doing.

—1 Thessalonians 5:11

Rules for Grandparents:
Never give your grandchildren
"candy and goodies" behind
their parents' backs.

*In everything set them an example by doing
what is good.*

—Titus 2:7

Rules for Grandparents:
Always remember to pray for your grandchildren.

Devote yourselves to prayer, keeping alert in it with an attitude of thanksgiving.

—Colossians 4:2 NASB

A Grandparent's Prayer

God, grant me the senility to forget
the people I dislike, the good fortune to
encounter those I like, and the eyesight
to be able to tell the difference.

*The LORD bless you and keep you; the LORD
make his face shine upon you and be gracious
to you; the LORD turn his face toward you and
give you peace.*

—Numbers 6:24-26

If you have enjoyed this book or it has
touched your life in some way,
Hallmark would like to hear from you.

Please send comments to

Book Feedback

2501 McGee, Mail Drop 250

Kansas City, MO 64141-6580

Or e-mail us at

booknotes@Hallmark.com